Do Commissions and Bo

Thomas Rittmannsberger

Do Commissions and Boni affect advisor behaviour?

An Online Experiment Using Amazon Mechanical Turk

Scholars' Press

Imprint

Any brand names and product names mentioned in this book are subject to trademark, brand or patent protection and are trademarks or registered trademarks of their respective holders. The use of brand names, product names, common names, trade names, product descriptions etc. even without a particular marking in this work is in no way to be construed to mean that such names may be regarded as unrestricted in respect of trademark and brand protection legislation and could thus be used by anyone.

Cover image: www.ingimage.com

Publisher:
Scholars' Press
is a trademark of
International Book Market Service Ltd., member of OmniScriptum Publishing Group
17 Meldrum Street, Beau Bassin 71504, Mauritius

Printed at: see last page
ISBN: 978-613-8-83768-8

Copyright © Thomas Rittmannsberger
Copyright © 2019 International Book Market Service Ltd., member of OmniScriptum Publishing Group

Acknowledgement

First I want to thank my professor, Markus Walzl for the helpful feedback throughout the planning and writing process. Furthermore, I very much thank the University of Innsbruck for granting me a performance-based scholarship. Without those funds I would not have been able to cunduct my experiment the way I did. Thank you very much!

Contents

Abstract

Modern households have a great responsibility to deal with their own saving and investment decisions. Unfortunately, since the financial market has become more sophisticated
and financial products more complex, investors usually lack the knowledge to meet these
challenges. Therefore, they increasingly rely on experts help to make investment decisions.
The information asymmetries, paired with the fact that financial advisors mostly rely on
incentive pay as their main source of income, can lead to inefficies in those markets, if those
incentive payments truely distort advisors' recommendations. In order to test, first, whether
advisors are receptive to different forms of incentive pay, namely commissions and bonus-
payments, and second, which of the two instruments is more effective in distorting advice,
I conduct an online experiment on the platform Amazon Mechanical Turk (MTurk). In
total 258 subjects participated in the experiment, while only 150 of them passed the control
questions and were therefore admitted to the final analysis. The result of the experiment are
very inconclusive. In general, the outcome of the experiment suggests using MTurk seems
not to be a appropriate tool for these kind of experiments, using a strategy method, since
participants do not pay sufficient attention to experimental instructions.

Zusammenfassung

Moderne Haushalte müssen immer mehr ihrer Spar- und Investmententscheidungen selbst treffen. Da die Finanzmärkte jedoch mittlerweile sehr hoch entwickelt sind, und Finanzprodukte immer komplexer werden, fehlt es den meisten Investoren an Wissen um dieser Aufgabe gerecht zu werden. Dementsprechend sind Investoren immer mehr von Experten abhängig, welche ihnen bei diesen Entscheidungen helfen sollen. Informationsasymmetrien in diesen Beziehungen, und die Tatsache, dass Finanzberater den größten Teil ihrer Einnahmen über Leistungsboni erhalten, können zu Ineffizienzen in diesen Märkten führen, falls sich die Art der Entlohnung eines Beraters auf dessen Empfehlung auswirkt. Diese Arbeit testet ob Berater für verschiedene Leistungsboni, sprich Kommissionen und Bonus-Zahlungen zugänglich sind. Weiteres wird untersucht welche der beiden Instrumente den größeren Einfluss auf die Beratungsqualität hat. Dafür wurde ein Online-Experiment auf der Platform Amazon Mechanical Turk (MTurk) durchgeführt. Insgesamt nahmen 258 Personen an dem Experiment teil, von denen jedoch nur 150 die Kontrollfragen richtig beantworteten und somit zur weiteren Analyse zugelassen wurden. Die Ergebnisse, welche das Experiment liefern sind wenig überzeugend. Insgesamt kann jedoch davon ausgegangen werden, dass MTurk nicht das Mittel der Wahl ist um solche Experimente, welche eine Abfrage mittels Strategiemethode durchführen.

1 Introduction

In recent years households have a greater responsibility to make their own saving and investment decisions and thereby actively manage their personal finances. At the same time the financial market has become more sophisticated, whereas most investors lack sufficient financial literacy. This combination nurtured the market for financial advice, which gained more and more importance in recent years. For example, about 73% of all investors in the United States consult a financial advisor before making a investment decision. (Hung, Clancy, Dominitz, Talley, Berrebi & Suvankulov, 2008).

Information asymmetries can become a huge problem in such markets, since advisor recommendations have a substantial influence on costumer behaviour (Beyer, de Meza & Reyniers , 2013; Reurink, 2018). The issue is reinforced since many financial advisors rely on commission payments as their main source of income (Hackenthal, Haliassos & Jappelli, 2008). Advisors do not necessarily recommend the adequate products for their costumers but instead those that are in line with their own financial interests (Mullainathan, Noeth and Schoar, 2012; Halan, Sane, 2016). Therefore, authorities have focussed on policy intervention targetting commission payments in those markets since they acknowledged that commissions played a vital role in the unfolding of the financial crisis of 2007/08 and the following European sovereign debt crisis. The main problem with commission is that they may distort advice, therefore reducing overall welfare (Inderst & Ottaviani, 2012a). Authorities around the world have passed laws to improve the functioning of financial markets and therefore strengthen investor protection.

On July 21, 2010 the United States US Ex-President Barack Obama signed the DoddFrank Wall Street Reform and Consumer Protection Act. Following MiFID (Markets in Financial Instruments Directive) which was in force from January 31, 2007 to January, 2 2018, the European Commission implemented MiFID II on January 3, 2018. Among other things it states that all kinds of commissions have to be disclosed, so that clients can understand the overall costs.

Generally speaking, financial advice can be seen as a credence good since the financial advisor does know more about the type of product the client needs than the client herself. Furthermore, since the outcome of most financial products are uncertain, it is almost impossible to link some *ex post* outcome of any financial product to a *ex ante* mistake of the advisor. That is, if some investment does not yield the expected payoff in the end, it is hard to tell whether this stems from bad advice or bad luck. In many cases, such as pension saving plans or life insurance, the benefits for the consumer becomes clear long after the purchase. Therefore, determining whether a certain product is beneficial for the consumer involves a lot of guesswork and speculation.

The existing literature is mainly concerned with commission payments and the effect disclosure has on market efficiency (Inderst & Ottaviani, 2012b, Inderst, 2015). It is assumed that (financial) advisors' recommendations react to different pay shemes and in the next step looked whether mandatory disclosure or other policy interventions, like caps on commissions, improves market welfare or consumer welfare. To my knowledge, there are few experiments that tried to investigate the pure effect that pay shemes have on advisor behaviour. Those experiments that were done included all parties and many variables. In my opinon it was hard to see any clear effects. By going one step back, this work tries to experimentally analyse the effect different pay shemes have on advisors recommendation.

1.1 Related Literature

In Dulleck and Kerschbaumer (2006) a general framework for analyzing markets for credence goods and expert providers is developed. They find that under certain conditions, verifiability and liability are sufficient conditions to enforce an efficient market. The reference market they use for their analysis is the market for car repair. Conducting an experiment, Dulleck, Kerschbaumer and Sutter (2011), however, do not find support for their theoretical finding. While the experimental market without verifiability performs better than predicted, verifiability seems not to bring the expected improvement. In Kerschbaumer, Sutter and Dulleck (2016) they conclude that social preferences seem to explain that discrepancy between theoretical prediction and empirical results. That is, whereas pro-social behaviour, like inequality aversion or striving for efficiancy does not improve the situation where actions are verifiable, market outcome is better under non-varifiable conditions. Anti-social behaviour on the other hand cannot worsen the already worst-case-scenario under non-varifiable conditions, however market outcome is worse with varifiability.

While their work contributes to a better understanding on the necessary institutions in credence good markets, their model differs from the world of financial advisors in some important ways. First, in their model the expert who provides the product is also the seller of the same, whereas in the case of financial advisors, they act as middleman between a firm and a costumer. Second, in Dulleck and Kerschbaumer (2006) the choice of the expert determines the outcome i. e. the payoff for the costumer. In financial markets, the outcome is somehow stochastic. While a financial advisor can recommend a product that seems suitable at the moment, she has no influence on the future development and therefore the returns of it.

Both these aspects are incorporated in the model of Inderst and Ottaviani (2012a). They develop a model of markets with advice, where they show how conflict of interest, created endogenously when firms compete over commissions, can distort advice and therefore lead to inefficient market outcomes. Within their framework they analyze the consequences of commonly adopted policies such as mandatory disclosure and caps on commissions.

Based on this model, Gottschalk (2018) experimentally analyses markets for financial advice. The main focus lies on analyzing the effect of disclosure and fines on advisors' recommendations, compared to a scenario of undisclosed commissions and uninformed consumers. Their experimental setting includes all parties, firms, advisors, and costumers, whereas one firm (firm A) is more cost-efficient than the other. Subjects in their experiment are assigned to matching groups of twelve players and play a one-shot-game for eight rounds. Participants were allotted one of four roles - firm A, firm B, advisor or consumer. Throughout the experiment matching groups and role assignments remain fixed. Within the matching groups, subjects are randomly matched before every round. At the first stage of their experiment the two firms independently set commissions. At the second stage firms observe all commissions in their group and independently choose product prices. In the third stage advisors get informed about prices and commissions. To elicit advisor behaviour a stragegy method is employed instead of asking advisors to make a decision at each possible probability, q. The probability $q \in [0, 1]$, which the advisor observes *ex ante*, captures the likelihood that product A is suitable. Advisors are asked at which cutoff they like to switch from recommending product B to recommending product A. In their experimental world the realization of q is restricted to eleven possibilities in ten percent-increments from zero to one. Advisors can chose among 23 possible strategies, since they can indicate that they are indifferent between recommending one or the other product at a chosen threshold. After observing the chosen advisors' strategies one scenario is randomly realized and the product the consumer requires is randomly determined based on the probabilities from the realizied scenario. At

3

the fourth stage the consumer is informed about the prices of the two product and the recommendation of the advisor. The consumer then chooses whether to buy the product of not.
If the consumer decides not to buy the product payoffs for all parties are zero. They find
that conflict of interest and biased advice arise endogenously in their experiment. Product
prices are lower and commissions are higher for firm A, due to the fact that it can produce
at lower costs than firm B. Interestingly, consumers in the experiment reject many of the
recommended products (42.4%).

While the experiments' results are generally in line with the theoretical analysis of Inderst
and Ottaviani (2012a) several questions are left unanswered, including the high rejection-
rate throughout all treatments. Furthermore, consumer welfare in unregulated markets is
already quite high, whereas it was predicted to be negative in this scenario. They conclude
that this outcome is most probabliy due to social preferances in the behaviour of firms,
advisors and consumers, especially inequity aversion.

In Honda and Inderst (2017) a new model is developed to analyze firms' competition to
steer advisors' recommendations through potentially non-linear incentives. The setting follows closely the model of Inderst and Ottaviani (2012a), however, in order to look at non-
linear incentives, a second costumer is introduced. The modelling framework is presented
in section 2. They find that even in the case of symmetric firms, where linear incentives
(commissions) do not lead to distortion of advice, advice is biased if those firms are allowed
to make compensation non-linear (bonus), which they optimally do. Furthermore, they find
that non-linear incentives seem to be more efficient than the same amount paid as linear
incentives.

The goal of this work is to experimentally analyze the market for advice, following the settig
of Honda & Inderst (2017) with two firms, one advisor, and two costumers. In order to do
so, I designed an online-experiment which I ran on the platform Amazon Mechanical Turk
(MTurk). It is important to note here, that I examine only the behaviour of the advisors
in this experiment. The firm is represented by some external fictitious entity that offers
commissions and boni to the advisors. No further information is revealed about the different firms. The costumer in this experiment is represented by a charity (A Childs Hope).
Participants are informed that the costumer buys the recommended product regardless of
the recommendation.

1.2 Amazon Mechanical Turk (MTurk)

Using Internet-based samples for data collection has become increasingly popular in many social science disciplines, including behaviral research. Amazon Mechanical Turk (MTurk) has attracted more and more attention of researchers over the last few years. It is a online data collection service run by Amazon.com that recruits research participants for (small) financial payments. The platform offers a wide range of possibilities for researchers to gather data, including runing experiments. Usually a requester creates a so called Human Intellegence Task (HIT), and pays a fixed amount of money to the worker for completing it. Additionally MTurk offers the possibility to reward workers with a bonus after completing the task.

Potential benefits of using online crowdsourcing platforms like MTurk are getting an easy accsess to a huge pool of patricipants for little money. However, there are many issues of concerns left. One of these is the question about the representativeness of the workers and the generalization of the obtained results.

In terms of location, 47% of MTurk workers are living in the United States, while about a third of them lives in India (Paolacci, Chandler & Ipeirotis, 2010). Comparing MTurk workers with the general US population, Ipeirotis (2010) finds that they have a similar income distribution (with a slightly lower mean) and are slightly younger. Additionally, MTurk workers tend to be better educated than the general population, although they are often unemployed or underemployed (Shapiro, Chandler & Mueller, 2013).

Another concern is the quality of the data. Workers typically only get small compensations for completing tasks, ranging from 0.01 USD per task to more than 10 USD. Compared to student-samples, which are very popular in research, it seems that samples obtained from MTurk offer a appropriate substitute with equal or even higher quality (Kees, Berry, Burton & Sheehan, 2017). However, since MTurk workers usually are at home when they are completing tasks, in contrast to students sitting in an controlled experimental environment, researchers worry that MTurk workers do not pay sufficient attention to study materials such as experiment descriptions. One easy way to have some degree of control over this challenge is to include control questions, so called instructional manipulation checks (IMC).

These IMC help researchers to check whether participants have understood the task at hand or not and may be used further to filter participants, therefore reducing statistical noise. Whereas there are many similarities between MTurk participants and traditional samples, they seem to be some important differences. Compared to student-samples, MTurk workers seem to pay less attention to experiment materials, reducing statistical power (Goodman, Cryder & Cheema, 2013).

While experiments on MTurk do not replace the high-quality field experiments in terms of external and ecological validity, they provide a useful alternative for survey experiments at lower costs and easier recruitment. (Paolacci et al., 2010; Stritch, Pedersen & Taggart, 2017; McCredie & Morey, 2018).

Based on the model of Honda and Inderst (2017) this work experimentally analyses the market of (financial) advice in an online-experiment using the crowdsourcing platform Amazon MTurk. In contrast to the work of Gottschalk (2018), this work focuses soleley on the advisors' behaviour, putting aside the decisions of the other market participants. Prices are fixed throughout the experiment and are equal for both firms, while commissions and boni of one firm are modified in the different treatments. The aim of this experiment is to get a better understanding if and how different pay shemes for advisors affect the quality of advice.

2 The Model

Since the model by Honda and Inderst (2017) is the base on which my experiment is built upon, it's key features are explained on the following pages.

The model considers firms' competition in providing incentives to advisors and serves as basis for the current experiment. The focus of the model is the analysis of different incentive shemes and its interaction with the suitability of advice. In this model, firms do not sell products directly to their costumers but do so indirecly through advisors. Non-advised sales do not arise in equilibrium.

Firms per-unit production costs are equal to c_n and the prices are equal to p_n.

Normalizing the utility of customers from not purchasing to zero, the utility of a given customer j from purchasing either product depends on a binary state variable $\theta \in \{A, B\}$ which captures the product's suitability, as follows: The customer derives utility $v_h > 0$ if the product matches the state and utility v_l otherwise, with $v_l < v_h$ (where v_l may be negative).

Advisor: One key feature of their model is that the advisor has some private information about the suitability of either product for a given costumer. Based on this private information, the advisors posterior belief is given by $q_j = Pr(\theta_j = A) \in [0, 1]$, which captures the likelihood that product A is suitable. q_j is *i.i.d.* with CDF $G(q_j)$ and density $g(q_j) > 0$ on $[0, 1]$.

Therefore the prior beliefs of all parties are: $Pr(\theta_j = A) = \int_0^1 qg(q)dq$ and $Pr(\theta_j = B) = \int_0^1 (1 - q)g(q)dq$.

Advisors are motivated by the (yet to be specified) incentive payments as well as by a preference for suitability of advice $\Delta w = w_h - w_l$. They derive utility w_h if the purchased product is suitable and w_l ($< w_h$) otherwise. In Inderst and Ottaviani (2012a) they develop three foundations for this suitability concern. The first one is, that advisors may be subject to a penalty, following inappropriate advice. In that case Δw captures the size of the fine that could be imposed by a regulator. The second foundation could be a reputation concern and the following loss of future business when giving unsuitable advice. Lastly Δw may capture the advisors professional concern for suitable advice, that is, the advisor cares about the well-being of the costumers.

When a customer does not purchase any of the two products, the advisor's utility (gross of any payments) is denoted by w_0. Assuming that $w_0 < w_l$, the advisor always recommends one of the two considered products, and thereby firms are always in competition through compensation. When making recommendations, the difference $w = w_h - w_l$ captures the advisors concern for the suitability of his recommendation. Despite his concern for the suitability of the advice, the advisor might make biased recommendations so as to receive higher payments from the firms, as described next. It is assumed that w is not too high and the advisor is suffiently responsive to pay schemes to make incentives worthwhile for firms. Below, a threshold for which this assumption holds is defined.

Compensation: Firms observe advisor's sales of their products and can thus make their incentive shemes contigent on that observation. Since advisors have an outside option of value zero firms have no incentive to pay a base salary.

To study whether advise is biased through different pay shemes it is sufficient to look at two costumers, so that $i = 1, 2$. In the following model firms have two option to compensate advisors for selling their product: *commissions* (f_n) and *boni* (b_n). Commissions are payed to the advisor whenever he sells a product, whereas boni are only payed to him if he sells the same product to both clients.

Timing: The timing for the model baseline analyisis is as follows:

$t = 1$: Firms simultaneously set their incentive shemes (f_n) and (b_n).

$t = 2$: Firms simultaneously set product prices p_n.

$t = 3$: The advisor provides advice to the first costumer, who then decides whether or not to purchase a single product. Subsequently this proces is repeated with the second costumer. The order of arrival is random and denoted by $i = 1, 2$, and custumers do not know whether they are first or second. The advisor privately observes product suitability q, for each costumers and advise is provided sending a message $m_i \in \{A, B\}$. Finally payoffs are realized.

For my following experiment only stage $t = 3$ is relevant and analyzed.

To undertand the pattern of advice the analysis starts by looking at the second costumer. If the advisor has sold product A to the first costumer, his expected payoff equals $f_A + b_A + q_2 w + w_l$ from recommending product A to the second costumer, whose observed product suitability is $q_2 \in [0, 1]$, and $f_B + (1 - q_2)w + w_l$ from recommending product B. Comparing those payoffs yields the threshold

$$\bar{q}_2^A = \frac{1}{2} - \frac{1}{2w}(f_A - f_B + b_A) \tag{1}$$

such that the advisor prefers to recommend product A if $q_2 \geq \bar{q}_2^A$ and product B otherwise. The subscript in $\bar{q}_2^A$ stands for the advice cutoff applied to the second arriving costumer, and the superscript indicates that product A has been sold to the first costumer already.

As for product A, similary the advisor, having sold product B to the first costumer, antici-
pates to receive $f_A + q_2 w + w_l$ from recommending product A to the second costumer, while
receiving $f_B + b_B + (1 - q_2)w + w_l$ for recommending product B. Again, comparing those
two payoffs yields

$$\bar{q}_2^B = \frac{1}{2} - \frac{1}{2w}(f_A - f_B + b_B) \tag{2}$$

such that the advisor prefers recommending product A if $q_2 \geq \bar{q}_2^B$ and product B otherwise.
The superscripts again indicates that product B has been sold to the first costumer already.

To deal with corner solutions $\bar{q}_2^A = 0$ if $w \leq f_A - f_B + b_A$ and $\bar{q}_2^A = 1$ if $w \leq -(f_A - f_B + b_A)$.
Similary $\bar{q}_2^B = 0$ if $w \leq f_A - f_B - b_B$ and $\bar{q}_2^B = 1$ if $w \leq -(f_A - f_B - b_B)$.

Now we look at the pattern of advice for the first costumer. Let

$$Z(\bar{q}_2^A) = \int_0^{\bar{q}_2^A} (f_B + (1 - q)w - w_l)g(q)dq + \int_{\bar{q}_2^A}^1 (f_A + b_A + qw + w_l)g(q)dq$$

and

$$Z(\bar{q}_2^B) = \int_0^{\bar{q}_2^B} (f_B + b_B + (1 - q)w + w_l)g(q)dq + \int_{\bar{q}_2^B}^1 (f_A + qw + w_l)g(q)dq.$$

Recommending product A to the first costumer with observed product suitability $q_1 \in$
$[0, 1]$, the advisor realizes $f_A + q_1 w + w_l + Z(\bar{q}_2^A)$, and recommending product B yields
$f_B + (1 - q)w + w_l + Z(\bar{q}_2^B)$.

Comparing those payoffs we get the threshold

$$\bar{q}_1 = \frac{1}{2} - \frac{1}{2w}(f_A - f_B + Z(\bar{q}_2^A) - Z(\bar{q}_2^B)), \tag{3}$$

such that the advisor prefers recommending product A if $q_1 \geq \bar{q}_1$ and recommending product
B otherwise. The subscript 1 in $\bar{q}_1$ stands for the advice cutoff applied to the first costumer.

To deal with corner solutions, $\bar{q}_1 = 0$ if $w \leq f_A - f_B + Z(\bar{q}_2^A) - Z(\bar{q}_2^B)$ and $\bar{q}_1 = 1$ if
$w \leq -(f_A - f_B + Z(\bar{q}_2^A) - Z(\bar{q}_2^B))$.

With the above analysis in mind, we can now characterize the pattern of advice for any given compensation plan (f_n, b_n).

3 Experiment

The aim of this paper is to test whether different pay shemes for advisors lead to a difference of the distortions of advice. Therefore, 9 different treatments are implemented in which the commissions and boni are modified. Table 1 shows the treatment and their payment structure.

3.1 Predictions and Hypothesis

Common sense already suggests the basic insights formally analyzed in Honda and Inderst (2017). First, more is always better. Therefore, a firms that offers higher commission payments than its competitors is more appealing to advisors, which in turn recommend that firms' products more offen. At least that's what is expected and hence the first hypothesis (H1) states that: *Higher commission payments of one firm leads to a biased advice towards this firms' products.*

To test this hypothesis the control treatment (CT) where both firms offer symmetric pay to their advisors ($f_A = f_B = 60ECU$; $b_A = b_B = 0ECU$) and three commission treatments (C2, C4, C7) are compared.

The same logic applies to bonus-payments. If both firms pay the same commissions and no bonus, Honda and Inderst (2017) already point out that it is optimal for a firm to offer a bonus, that makes recommendation of the second costumer contingent on the first costumers recommendation. Increasing bonus-payment even further is expected to bias advice further towards that firms' products. Therefore, the second hypothesis (H2) states that: *Higher bonus payments of one firm lead to biased advice towards that firms' products.*

To test this hypothesis the control treatment (CT), where both firms offer symmetric pay and no bonus to their advisors ($f_A = f_B = 60ECU$; $b_A = b_B = 0ECU$) is compared to the five bonus treatments (B3, B4, B5, B7, B14).

10

The argument for the first two hypothesis is very easy to retrace, since it should be clear that if any firm offers more money to advisors than its competitors, advisors will react by recommending that firms' products more often in order to enrich themselves (unless advisors value *honest advice* more than the financial incentive).

It's getting more interesting when looking at the comparisson between commissions and bonus-payments. Whereas firms can safely assume that paying higher incentives increases their sales (if advisors are receptive to them), it is not clear which of the two instruments should be choosen. A firm can either chose to increase commission payments by x or increase bonus payments by $2x$. In the end, if both consumers get recommended its product they end up paying the same amount of money. Honda and Inderst (2017) give a relatively clear answer to that question. Using the model to predict the distortion of advice for either the commission or the bonus shows that increasing the bonus by any amount seems to distort advisors behavour more than increasing the commission payment by the matching amount. This effect is more pronounced the higher the increase gets. The third hypothesis (H3) hence states: *Paying the same amount of money as commissions or boni leads to stronger distortion of advice for boni.*

To test this hypothesis commission and bonus treatments are compared pairwise (C2 with B4, C4 with B8, and C7 with B14).

If bonus-payments are truly more effective in distorting advisors behaviour than commissions, firms should use smaller increases in bonus payments, compared to higher increases in commissions payments. The fourth hypothesis (H4) therefore is: *The same distortion of advice is reached by a smaller bonus compared to a higher commission.*

To test this hypothesis, again commission and bonus treatments are compared pairwise (C2 with B3, C4 with B5, and C7 with B8).

3.2   Experiment Implementation

The experiment was carried out on the 5th of November, 2018 on the crowdsourcing Internet marketplace Amazon Mechanical Turk (MTurk). The goal was to get 150 observations.

11

At the beginning of the experiment participants were given a short introduction (Appendix). They where informed about the procedere of the experiment and all the relevant features (payoff structures, experimental process, etc.). MTurk requires to offer a fixed reward for completing the experiment, however offers a possibility to reward participants after completing the survey with a bonus-payment. Note that this bonus-payment does not refer to the bonus in the experiment. Since my experiment needs to offer financial incentives to the participants, they were informed in the first paragraph that the acutal payment they receive depends on the choices they make throughout the experiment. They were informed about the fact that they must answer five control questions in order to be accepted to the experiment. I made it very clear that only workers who answered those five control questions correctly would be part of the experiment and therefore receive payment.

The five *multiple coice* control questions tested whether the participants understood the design and procedure of the following experiment. The first question was "*How many costumers do I meet one after another in each game?*" and they the possible answers were 2, 3, 4, with 2 being the right answer. Questions two and three checked if the patricipant understood the payoff structure. The second question "*How much does a type A costumer receive if you advise her to buy product A?*" and the third "*How much does a type A costumer receive if you advise her to buy product B?*" had the same possilbe answers (30, 60, 120, 180, 240, and 300 ECU). The right answer for the second question was 240 ECU and for the third 60 ECU. Question four and five tested whether subjects were aware of the difference between commissions and boni and their consequences for advisor payoffs. Question four asked "*What is a commission?*". Two answers, "A commission is payed to me whenever I advice my costumer to by a product." and "A commission is payed to me whenever I advice my first, as well as my second costumer to buy the product from the same firm." were possible, with the first one beeing the right one. The same was done in the last control question "*What is a bonus?*". The answeres were the same with "bonus" instead of "commission" in the answer-text, therefore the second answer was the right one.

After completing these control questions, participants started with the actual experiment. Unfortunately, MTurk does not provide the possibility to stop subjects right after giving false answers on (at least one) of the control questions. Therefore, participants completed the whole experiment even if they already failed at the control questions.

The following experiment was organized in three sections. The first section concerned the first costumer, the other two the second costumer.

Following Gottschalk (2018) I employed a strategy method to elict the advisors' behaviours. The advisor in this experiment is asked to reveal his full strategy and I can hence directly determine the advisor's cutoff. In order to keep the task simple for subjects, I implemented monotonic switching as I asked advisors at which threshold they like to switch from recommending product B to recommending product A, rather than asking them to make a decision at each possible probability q_j. The question was always stated as "*Decide at which threshold you are about to recommend product A to your costumer!*"

With respect to the probability q_j, I restricted the experimental world to eleven possible relaizations in ten percent-increments from zero to one, $0\%, 10\%, \ldots 90\%, 100\%$, representing a discrete version of the signal from the continous model presented in section 2. Advisors decide up to which threshold they recommend product B and starting from which they recommend product A. At the chosen threshold advisors are indifferent to recommending either product. That is, choosing a threshold of e.g. $\bar{q}_1 = 0.6$ means that every costumer with $q < 0.6$ gets recommended product B, every costumer with $q > 0.6$ product A. Costumers with $q = 0.6$ get either product A or product B with equal probability.

All advisors can therefore chose among 11 possible strategies (table 2).

In every section (first costumer, second costumer (first A), second costumer (first B)), subjects were asked to reveal their chosen threshold for the nine different treatments (table 1). The difference between the treatments concerned the incentives offered to the advisor by the two firms. In the control treatment, both firms offered a commission of 60 ECU and zero bonus. In the three commission-treatments, the commission payment of firm A increased. In the five bonus-treatments, the offered bonus of firm A increased. The smallest bonus offered was 3 ECU, the highest 14 ECU. Throughout all the experimental-treatments (commission- and bonus-treatments) the compensation plan of firm B did not change.

In total subjects had to answer 32 questions (5 control questions and 27 experimental questions). The order of the questions was the same for every participant. After competing the control questions, subjects were asked to reveal their threshold for the control treatment,

13

then the three commission treatments (C2, C4, and C7), followed by the bonus-treatments (B4, B8, B14, B3, B5).

The question was always asked in the same manner. For example, the question in the second section for the B4-treatment was:

Decide at which threshold you are about to recommend product A to your second costumer!

Firm A pays a commission of $c(A) = 60ECU$ and a bonus of $b(A) = 4ECU$
Firm B pays a commission of $c(B) = 60ECU$ and a bonus of $b(B) = 0ECU$

Below that question, subjects had to chose a threshold on the interval $q \in [0, 1]$ in ten percent increments. In the appendix, figure 2 shows a screenshot of two questions from the first section.

After the fist section, participants were informed that the following questions concerned the second costumer. Furthermore, they were informed before the second section that the first costumer already got product A, and before the third section that the first costumer already got product B. ("*In the following nine questions you have to reveal your threshold of recommending product A to your second costumer, provided having recommended product [...] to your first client!* ").

As soon as the submission was finished the 150 valid observations were filtered out in order to transfer their payments. At the beginning of the next section I describe how this filtering was done. The payment to the 150 accepted participants was transfered on the 6th of November, 2018. In total USD 377.64 (EUR 359.60) were transfered to Amazon Mechanical Turk out of which USD 289.70 (EUR 275.80) were payed to the subjects of the experiment. The rest USD 87.94 (EUR 83.60) had to be payed to MTurk as fees in order to use their platform.

The payment of USD 463.5 (EUR 418.30) to the fictitious consumer, the charity "A Childs Hope" was made on the 30th of December, 2018.

3.3   Data preperation

Amazon MTurk closes the survey after the aimed for observations are finished. Therefore, I had to check the control question of every subject before accepting it, rejecting those who had at least one wrong answer in the control-section. After rejecting participants, MTurk fills up with fresh observation. After several rounds of accepting and rejecting, the goal of 150 (valid) obervations was reached. In total 258 observatoions were submitted, with 108 of them having incorrect answers in the control questions. The average completion time for the 258 observation was 9:24 minutes, for the accepted 150 observations it was 10:15 minutes.

The further analysis of the data was done using the software package IBM SPSS Statistics 20.

To test differences between treatments I rely on non-parametric tests, Kruskal-Wallis and Mann-Whitney-U (MWU), since the observed data was not normal-distributed as shown by the applied Kolmogorov-Smirnov-Test.

In order to look whether subjects did understand the experimental setting I furthermore looked at the acumulated frequencies of observed thresholds for $q \in [0, 0.5]$. Additionally I checked whether or not a participant ever chose a threshold $q > 0.5$.

4   Results

Although the analysis of the observed data has been done and is presented in the following pages, I must clarify that the quality of the data seems not to be as good hoped for. The limitations of this study are presented and discussed later.

First Hypothesis: In order to test the H1, I looked at the four commission-treatments (CT, C2, C4, C7) to see whether or not there is a difference between them. The Kruskal-Wallis-Test shows that there is a difference between at least two treatments for the first costumer, $H(8) = 25.77$, $p < 0.05$, and the second customer, if the first costumer already bought product, $H(8) = 25.08$, $p < 0.05$. For the second costumer, conditional on having sold product A to the first one, there is no significant difference between the four commission-treatments, $H(8) = 12.41$, $p > 0.1$.

To follow up this result three Mann-Whitney-U-Tests were conducted (CT vs. C2, C2 vs.

C4, C4 vs C7). A Bonferroni correction was applied and so all effects are reported at a 0.0167 level of significance. For the first costumer there is a significant difference between CT and C2 ($U = 7125$, $r = -0.26$). However, looking at the mean values one can see that the applied threshold for CT was $\bar{q}_{1\_(CT)} = 0.50$ while for C2 it was $\bar{q}_{1\_(C2)} = 0.56$. There seems to be no significant differences neither between C2 and C4 ($U = 8746$, $r = -0.03$) nor between C4 and C7 ($U = 8139$, $r = -0.12$).

There is no significant difference of advice for the second costumer, conditional on having sold product A to the first one. The closest to significance was the comparisson between CT and C2, $U = 7760$, $r = -0.170$, with a significance level $p < 0.05$, however not falling below the Bonferroni correction applied.

For the second costumer, conditional on having sold product B to the first costumer, there were no significant differences between neither CT and C2 ($U = 7616$, $r = -0.190$), C2 and C4 ($U = 8707$, $r = -0.04$), nor C4 and C7 ($U = 8859$, $r = -0.02$) at the significant level of 0.0167.

The hypothesis that higher commission payments of one firm leads to biased advice towards that firms' product, is rejected on grounds of the carried out experiment.

Second Hypothesis: To test whether higher bonus payments of one firm lead to distortion of advice towards that firms product, I compared the different bonus treatments with each other.

The Kruskal-Wallis-Test shows that there is a difference between at least two treatments for all the three different scenarios. First costumer, $H(8) = 20.28$, $p < 0.01$. Second costumer conditional on having sold product A to the first one, $H(8) = 9.55$, $p < 0.05$. Second costumer conditional on having sold product B to the first one, $H(8) = 23.23$, $p < 0.01$.

To follow up this result three Mann-Whitney-U-Tests were conducted (CT vs.B4, B4 vs. B8, B8 vs B14). A Bonferroni correction was applied and so all effects are reported at a 0.0167 level of significance. Table 5 shows the results of the three MTU-Tests.

There seems to be a significant difference between CT and B4 for the first costumer ($U = $

7339, $r = -0.232$), as well as for the second costomer, conditional on having sold product B to the first ($U = 7378$, $r = -0.223$). For the second scenario, that is, second costumer conditional on having sold product A to the first one, there is no significant difference between CT and B4 at a 0.0167 level of significance, $U = 7742$, $r = -0.172$.

Comparing the chosen thresholds in the two significant scenarios shows that the threshold was higher in both bonus-treatments than in the control-treatments.

Comparing B4 with B8 shows no significant differences between the two in any of the three scenarios. The same is true for the comparisson of B8 with B14. It seems that only going from offering *no bonus* to offering *some bonus* leads to different distortion of advice, however increasing the bonus further does not distort advice any more. Furthermore, looking at the chosen thresholds, it seems that offering a bonus to the advisors distorts advice towards the firms' product that *does not* offer a bonus, clearly contradicting the predicted direction.

The hypothesis that higher bonus payments of one firm leads to biased advice towards that firms'product, is rejected on grounds of the carried out experiment.

Third Hypothesis: To test H3, which states that the same amount paid as bonus leads to greater advisor bias than the equivalent commission, the three commission-treatments C2, C4, and C7 are compared with the bonus-treatments B4, B8, and B14, using three Mann-Whitney-U-Tests (Table 6).

The advice does not differ significantly between paying 2 ECU in commission compared to paying 4 ECU in bonus, for neither the first ($U = 8749$, $r = -0.032$), nor the second costumer, regardless of the advice for the first costumer (First A: $U = 8731$, $r = -0.033$; First B: $U = 8695$, $r = -0.039$). Looking at the difference between C4 and B8, there seems to be a significant difference only for the first costumer ($U = 7741$, $r = -0.162$).

Paying 7 ECU in commission compared to 14 ECU in bonus does change the pattern of advice weakly significantly only for the second costumer if the first one already got product B, $U = 7868$, $r = -0.153$

It seems, that in this experiment linear commission payments are as effective as nonlinear

17

bonus payments. *The hypothesis, paying a matching amount as bonus instead of paying a commission leads to a stronger distortion of advice is rejected on grounds of the carried out experiment.*

Forth Hypothesis: Finally, testing whether achieving the same distortion of advice can be reached by paying an amout as bonus that is smaler than the matching commission, I look once more at the three commission-treatments, however comparing them with B3, B5 and B7. Based on the insights of the model, there should be no difference in the pattern of advice for those comparrisons.

The three Mann-Whitney-U-Tests support the hypothesis: There is no significant difference of advice for neither the first, nor the second costumer, regardless of the product sold to the first client (Table 7). The same distortion of advice is reached by offering a bonus that is less than what the two commission payments amount to.

The data here suggests that bonus payments are in fact more effective than commissions. A firm paying a smaller amount to its advisors in boni reaches the same distortion of advice than paying a higher amount in commissions. *The experiment hence supports the hypothesis that bonus payments are more effective than commissions.*

Clearly, there must be something off here. Whereas Hypothesis 3 is rejected on grounds of the present experiment, Hypothesis 4 would be supported. However, both state that bonus payments are more effective than commissions. In the following section I will try to explain the problems which may be the basis for this strange inconsitency.

5 Discussion

The aim of this experiment was to look whether different pay shemes for advisors lead to different distortion of advice. In order to do that, an online experiment was conducted on the online crowdsourcing platform Amazon MTurk. A total of 258 observations were submitted, however only 150 of those correctly answered the five control questions and hence were admitted to the final analysis.

Looking at the results it is clear that Hypothesis 1 and Hypothesis 2 are rejected. That is, participants in this experiment were not influenced by different pay shemes. Increasing the commission of one firm did not lead to a greater advisor bias towards that firms' products, nor was it the case with bonus payments. Although there there seems to be that advisor chose a different threshold, whenever one firm left the symmetric situation. That is, offering a higher commission payment, as well as introducing a bonus, did change the pattern of advice compared to the control-treatment. However, further increasing either the commission or the bonus did not change advisors behavior.

Furthermore, even for the cases where the chosen threshold was different, the direction contradicts not only the model-predcition but also common sese. In this experiment the firm that deviated from the symmetric situation was punished by the advisors. A firm deciding to offer either a higher commission payment than its competitor or introducing a bonus payment lead to less advisors' recommendations of that firms product. Whereas, not responding to the offered incentives could be explained by advisors concern for fairness of advice, recommeinding less products of the firm offering more incentive does not make much sense in this setting.

This result is clearly in contrast to the work of Gottschalk (2018). In his experiment, where one firm had a cost-advantage, and therefore was able to offer higher commissions to the advisors, advice was systematicaly biased towards that firms' products. However, in my view, the results of his experiment are difficult to interpret, especially because of the asymmetric cost structure for the two firms. The more cost-efficient firms could offer higher commissions *and* lower prices. Therefore, the effects of higher commissions are not clear. Furthermore, the focus of their work was to examine the effects of policy interventions and compared their results with the predictions from the model of Inderst and Ottaviani (2012a). Participants in the experiment held all the roles (firm, advisor, and consumer), compared to my experiment, where I looked solely on advisors behaviour and the effects that different pay shemes have on advice. Both the firms and the consumer were external entities.

Looking at the difference between commissions and boni opens many questions. Only the first costumer got a significant different advice when comparing the two treatments C4 and B8. Not only is it incosistent with the model-prediction, I cannot come up with any reasoning supporting this finding. Especially the case, where the first client already bought product A, and firm A offers a bonus for selling the same product to another costumer, one would expect to see a distortion of advice towards that firms product. However, not only did the recommendation for the second costumer not change in the different treatments, looking at the mean values of the chosen threshold reveals that the direction of distortion show in exactly the different direction than the model predicts. Throughout the experiment, the chosen advisors' cutoffs where higher in the bonus-treatments than in the commission-treatments. Looking at the most extreme scenario, comparing C7 with B14, the model by Honda and Inderst (2017) predicts a cutoff for the first, as well as for the second costumer (conditional on having sold product A to the first costumer) close to *zero* for the bonus-treatments, compared to 0.27 for the commission-treatment. Though, in this experiment there seems not to be any significant difference between those two. Clearly there is some other factor at play here.

The results of testing hypothesis 3 suggest that the effectiveness of distorting advice using commissions is the same as using boni. Looking at the results for testing H4 tells a different story though. Advisor bias there was the same when paying a smaller bonus than the two commission payments would amount to. Even for the most extreme comparison, comparing C7 to B8, advisors' recommendations did not change in any of the three scenarios. Although this result is consistent with the model-prediction, the credebility of it should be questioned very carefully, as discussed in the next section.

Looking at the results from this experiment, there seem to be many inconsistencies not only with the predictions from the model by Honda and Inderst (2017), but also with common sense. Whether these results should be given any credence at all, it is a good idea to look at the shortcommings and limitations hopefully finding some clarification.

5.1 Limitations

Going through the literature, there may be many possible explainations for the (strange) experimental outcome.

One of those might be, that the decisions made by the experimental participants was driven by concerns of pro-social behaviour rather than the financial incentives (Fehr & Schmidt, 1999; Dulleck & Kerschbaumer, 2018). Advisors in the experiment did not react to the financial incentives as predicted by the theory. In most cases the reported advice-cutoff did not change if the commissions or the boni were increased. This concern for fairness may be appreciated even further in this experiment, due to the chosen payoff structure. The financial incentive for the advisors was only small compared to the losses the consumer would occur when buying a inappropriate product. Gettig recommended the wrong product, and buying it, would leave the client worse of by 150 ECU ($ 1.50), whereas the potential gain for the advisor would range only from 4 ECU ($ 0.03) to 14 ECU ($ 0.12). This explanaition is consistent with Horton et al. (2011), who find that MTurk participants have pro-social preferences.

In the theoretical model, this concern is represented by the *preference for suitability of advice*, which is defined as the difference between w_h and w_l. This difference Δw in advisors utility may occour through different channels as discussed in section 2. Since my experimental setting does not impose any penalty on the advisor for wrong advice, nor does the advisor have to care about future payoff-losses, the most plausible explaination left is the *proffessional concern* for suitable advice. When predicting the experimental-outcomes, I assumed the concern for suitable advice to be $\Delta w = 15 ECU$. The reason for this was to leave the advisors sufficiently responsive to pay shemes.

The responsiveness to pay shemes, however, may not be sufficient in the present experiment. This is another limitation that should be acknowledged. Not only were the financial incentives in this experiment quite small compared to the potential losses of consumers due to bad advice, they were further quite small compared to the *base salary* the advisors obtained. Participants may perceive an extra 2 ECU ($ 0.02) in commission, compared to 60 ECU ($ 0.50), they earn anyway, regardless of their choice, as just too little. Whereas the model predicts strong responsiveness to already quite small financial incentives, one should acknowledge that these incentives may not trigger the expected action.

Looking at the results, to me it seems that it was neither the concern for fairness and equality, nor the lack of responsiveness to financial incentives that drove participants' decisions. I rather think, that the underlying problem was that participants did not pay sufficient attention to the task at hand, either due to a general lack of interest or a problem with comprehending the experimental instructions.

To gauge whether participants pay attention, I implemented five control questions that had to be answered correctly in order to be accepted to the experiment. Participants who did not answer those questions correctly still finished the experiment, however, their answeres were not part of the final analysis. The goal was to gather 150 observations, since I expected already to have some statistical noise. In total 258 participants took part in the experiment, 108 (42 %) of them failing at the control questions. To be honest, this came to me as a surprise, since the control questions were only checking whether one had read the instructions carefully. Furthermore, all the participants in this study were new to MTurk and my experiment was the first survey they ever did on the platform. Having such a high number of rejections suggests that pre-selecting participants would have been a good idea. Although MTurk offers the option to recruit only workers with a documented history of good performance, I did not use any restrictions on the basis of approval rate for the present study, following McCredie and Morey (2018). For future experiments I would probably make use of this instrument in order to ensure to include only experienced workers.

However, since only the participants who succeeded at the control questions were analyzed in the end, having such a high number of rejections cannot be the explaination for the experimental results in the end.

Accepting only workers who answered the five control questions correctly did ensure that those participants read the instructions. However, it did not guarantee that they really comprehended the structure of the experiment, especially the strategy method. While it was easy to implement it, the results suggest that the reliability of the strategy method in this study should be rejected. This is due to two arguments.

First, using the stragegy method made the survey monotone and probably boring for the participants. Having in mind, that MTurk workers report completing tasks not only to receive extra income, but also out of enjoyment (Paolacci et al., 2010), one might expect that having to chose a cutoff 27 times does not evoke much euphoria. It might therefore be advisable to ask participants to reccommend products to concrete consumers instead of asking them to reveal a strategy. To make the task even easier, one might imagine to implement a graphic representation of the consumers type. This leads already to the second argument.

Even if participants generally understood the structure of the experiment, chosing thresholds in the different scenarios still demanded some degree of abstract and strategic thinking.

22

In my opinion, this is the main reason for the obtained results. Whereas most of the differences in cutoffs were not significant anyway, those that were contradiccted the predicted direction. Whereas social preferences, such as inequity aversion (Fehr & Schmidt, 1999) may be at play, such that advisors punish the firm that deviates from a symmetric scenario by eigher paying higher commissions or boni, it is not very plausible giving the experimental structure. Participents were informed about the fact that only they are actively taking part in the experiment. Furthermore, only the participants and a third party, the consumer (represented by a charity) would receive any payments in the end. Strategic punishment of a deviating firm therefore seems unrealistic. Especially because the game is played only once.

Having this in mind, it seems clear that chosing any threshold $\bar{q}$ above 0.5 is a sign for not comprehending the experiment. Even for the case where participants are completely immune to any offered financial incentives, one should observe a threshold $\bar{q} = 0.5$. Whenever participants are prone to financial incentives the chosen cutoff should lie somewhere between $\bar{q} \in [0, 0.5]$.

Looking at the accumulated frequencies of advice in the last column of table 3 one can see that for most cases the above reasoning does not apply. For the most part of the experiment, only about half of the observed thresholds were in the reasonable range. This finding calls the reliability of the obtained results into question.

To further check if participants really understood the experiment and the strategy method I looked at the revealed stragegy of all participants in all different scenarios. Since every participant could choose out of eleven possible strategies (table 2) I looked for those participants who only chose among the six feasable strategies with $\bar{q} \in [0, 0.5]$. Out of the 150 participants who took part in the experiment and correctly answered the five control questions, only six never chose a threshold above $\bar{q} = 0.5$.

6   Conclusion

The goal of this study was to get a better understanding on the effect different pay shemes have on the quality of advice. In order to do so an online experiment was conducted on the 15th of November, 2018 on the the crowdsourcing Internet marketplace Amazon Mechanical Turk (MTurk). The theoretical base for the experiment was the work of Inderst and Ottaviani (2012a) and Honda and Inderst (2017). In Inderst and Ottaviani (2012a), the authors develop a model to look at the effects linear financial incentives in form of commissions have on the quality of advice and find that higher commission payments of one firm lead to biased advice toward that firm's products. Honda and Inderst (2017) develop a model to analyze the effects of non-linear financial incentives in form of boni on advisor bias and they find that boni lead to strong distortions of advice, and seem to be more effective than commissions.

The current experiment tests these theories and finds none of the anticipated effects. Neither do higher commission or higher bonus payments lead to increased advisor bias, nor are non-linear bonus payments more effective in distorting advice than linear commission payments. Advisors behaviour remained more or less the same throughout all the different treatments and did not respond to different financial incentives.

Looking at the limitations and shortcommings of the experiment it seems clear that participants did not sufficiently comprehend the task they were asked to perform, even though, five control questions had to be answered correctly which verified that participants carefully read the instructions. It seems that the applied strategy method, which was also used in Gottschalk (2018) in a similar, but more extensive experiment, was the biggest problem in getting reliable results. Instead of asking the participants to make a decision for different costumers, they were asked to reveal their full strategy. Therefore, they were asked to chose a cutoff-value at which they indicated indifference between recommending either product A or product B. In total they had to chose a cutoff for three different scenarios in one control-treatment and eight experimental-treatments. In the control treatment both firms offered the same commissions and no bonus. The experimental-treatments were charactarized by one firm paying either higher commissions or higher boni. The three scenarios were as follows. First they had to decide a cutoff for the first consumer, then for the second, conditional on having sold either product A or the product B to the first costumer. In total they had to chose a cutoff 27 times.

Not only did the results of this strategy method reveal almost no significant differences, compared to the predictions, in the few cases where a significant difference was observed, the direction of the difference was not only counterintuitive, but also contradicted the theoretical predictions. Checking the given answeres, especially looking at chosen cutoffs that make no sense, the present work leads to the conclusion that a strategy method should not be applied, using the online platform Amazon Mechanical Turk, unless some restrictions for participating in the experiment are implemented *ex ante*.

7 Tables

Experimental Treatments

Treatment	f_A	f_B	b_A	b_B
CT	60	60	0	0
C2	62	60	0	0
C4	64	60	0	0
C7	67	60	0	0
B3	60	60	3	0
B4	60	60	4	0
B5	60	60	5	0
B8	60	60	8	0
B14	60	60	14	0

Table 1: There is one control treatment (CT) where both firms offer symmetric pay to their advisors. In the eight experimental treatments the commissions and boni of firm A (f_A, b_A) are modified. The eight experimental treatments are divided into thre commission-treatments and four bonus-treatments.

Possible strategy choices of advisors

#	0%	10%	20%	30%	40%	50%	60%	70%	80%	90%	100%
1	A/B	A	A	A	A	A	A	A	A	A	A
2	A	A/B	A	A	A	A	A	A	A	A	A
3	A	A	A/B	A	A	A	A	A	A	A	A
4	A	A	A	A/B	A	A	A	A	A	A	A
5	A	A	A	A	A/B	A	A	A	A	A	A
6	A	A	A	A	A	A/B	A	A	A	A	A
7	A	A	A	A	A	A	A/B	A	A	A	A
8	A	A	A	A	A	A	A	A/B	A	A	A
9	A	A	A	A	A	A	A	A	A/B	A	A
10	A	A	A	A	A	A	A	A	A	A/B	A
11	A	A	A	A	A	A	A	A	A	A	A/B

Table 2: The eleven possible strategies an advisor can chose from.

First Costumer				
Treatment	$\overline{q}_{1\_pred}$	$\overline{q}_{1\_exp}$	$\Delta\overline{q}_1$	σ	$\sum_{q=0}^{0.5} R_{\overline{q}_{1\_exp}}$
CT	0.50	0.50	0.00	0.267	0.77
C2	0.43	0.58	0.15	0.256	0.49
C4	0.37	0.57	0.20	0.276	0.51
C7	0.27	0.62	0.35	0.281	0.45
B3	0.44	0.60	0.16	0.291	0.51
B4	0.42	0.60	0.18	0.294	0.42
B5	0.39	0.63	0.24	0.272	0.41
B8	0.29	0.63	0.34	0.283	0.47
B14	0.05	0.65	0.60	0.301	0.48

Second Costumer: first costumer got product A				
Treatment	$\overline{q}_{2\_pred}^{A}$	$\overline{q}_{2\_exp}^{A}$	$\Delta\overline{q}_2^{A}$	σ	$\sum_{q=0}^{0.5} R_{\overline{q}_{2\_exp}^{A}}$
CT	0.50	0.50	0.00	0.292	0.72
C2	0.43	0.56	0.13	0.289	0.52
C4	0.37	0.55	0.18	0.297	0.53
C7	0.27	0.58	0.31	0.298	0.49
B3	0.40	0.58	0.18	0.298	0.52
B4	0.37	0.59	0.22	0.295	0.52
B5	0.33	0.60	0.27	0.295	0.52
B8	0.23	0.60	0.37	0.305	0.46
B14	0.03	0.62	0.59	0.328	0.43

Second Costumer: first costumer got product B				
Treatment	$\overline{q}_{2\_pred}^{B}$	$\overline{q}_{2\_exp}^{B}$	$\Delta\overline{q}_2^{B}$	σ	$\sum_{q=0}^{0.5} R_{\overline{q}_{2\_exp}^{B}}$
CT	0.50	0.42	0.00	0.298	0.80
C2	0.43	0.50	0.13	0.308	0.62
C4	0.37	0.52	0.15	0.314	0.58
C7	0.27	0.52	0.25	0.311	0.56
B3	0.50	0.51	0.01	0.302	0.58
B4	0.50	0.52	0.02	0.294	0.60
B5	0.50	0.54	0.04	0.299	0.56
B8	0.50	0.57	0.07	0.310	0.50
B14	0.50	0.59	0.09	0.335	0.49

Table 3: $\overline{q}_{1\_pred}$, $\overline{q}_{2\_pred}^{A}$ and $\overline{q}_{2\_pred}^{B}$ are the predicted thresholds following the model of Honda and Inderst (2017). $\overline{q}_{1\_exp}$, $\overline{q}_{2\_exp}^{A}$ and $\overline{q}_{2\_exp}^{B}$ are the mean values of the 134 observations in the different treatments. The difference between the experiment outcomes and the predicted values is given as $\Delta\overline{q}$. The fourth column shows the standard deviation of the mean σ. The last column tells us the acumulated frequencies of observed thresholds for $q \in [0, 0.5]$.

Results: Hypothesis 1
(n = 134)

	First Costumer					
	CT	C2	C2	C4	C4	C7
$\bar{q}_{1\_exp}$	0.5	0.58	0.58	0.57	0.57	0.62
s	0.267	0.256	0.256	0.276	0.276	0.281
U		7125		8746		8139
r		-0.263		-0.032		-0.115
p		0.002**		0.711		0.182
	Second Costumer: first costumer got product A					
	CT	C2	C2	C4	C4	C7
$\bar{q}^{A}_{2\_exp}$	0.5	0.55	0.56	0.55	0.55	0.58
s	0.292	0.289	0.289	0.297	0.297	0.298
U		7760		8656		8336
r		-0.170		-0.044		-0.088
p		0.049**		0.609		0.310
	Second Costumer: first costumer got product B					
	CT	C2	C2	C4	C4	C7
$\bar{q}^{B}_{2\_exp}$	0.44	0.50	0.50	0.52	0.52	0.52
s	0.298	0.308	0.308	0.314	0.314	0.311
U		7616		8707		8859
r		-0.190		-0.037		-0.016
p		0.028**		0.667		0.851

Table 4: The carried out MWU-Test shows, that paying a higher commission distorts advice only for the first time a firm increases its' commission payments (CT vs. C2) in all three scenarios. Increasing commissions further does not lead to a different advisor bias (C2 vs. C4 and C4 vs. C7). However, looking at the direction of distortion, one can see that the threshold is higher in C2 than it is in CT. On the basis of this test, one can clearly reject Hypothesis 1. Higher commission payments of one firm **do not** lead to a stronger bias towards that firms' products. s revers to the standard deviation of the chosen threshold, r is the effect size $r = \frac{Z}{\sqrt{n}}$, and p is the significance level (*: $p < 0.1$, **: $p < 0.05$).

Results: Hypothesis 2
(n = 134)

First Costumer					
	CT	B4	B4	B8	B8	B14
$\bar{q}_{1\_exp}$	0.5	0.60	0.60	0.63	0.63	0.65
s	0.267	0.294	0.294	0.283	0.283	0.301
U		7339		8266		8695
r		-0.232		-0.098		-0.039
p		0.007**		0.256		0.651
Second Costumer: first costumer got product A						
	CT	B4	B4	B8	B8	B14
$\bar{q}_{2\_exp}^{A}$	0.5	0.59	0.59	0.60	0.60	0.62
s	0.292	0.295	0.295	0.305	0.305	0.328
U		7742		8739		8642
r		-0.172		-0.033		-0.046
p		0.047**		0.704		0.594
Second Costumer: first costumer got product B						
	CT	B4	B4	B8	B8	B14
$\bar{q}_{2\_exp}^{B}$	0.44	0.52	0.52	0.57	0.57	0.59
s	0.298	0.294	0.294	0.310	0.310	0.335
U		7378		8079		8537
r		-0.223		-0.124		-0.061
p		0.010**		0.153		0.483

Table 5: The carried out MWU-Test shows, that paying a bonus distorts advice only for the first time a firm introduces the bonus (CT vs. B4) in all three scenarios. Increasing the bonus further does not lead to a different advisor bias (B4 vs. B8 and B8 vs. C14). However, looking of the direction of distortion, one can see that the threshold is higher in B2 than it is in CT. On the basis of this test, one can clearly reject Hypothesis 2. Higher bonus payments of one firm **do not** lead to a stronger bias towards that firms' products. s revers to the standard deviation of the chosen threshold, r is the effect size $r = \frac{Z}{\sqrt{n}}$, and p is the significance level (*: $p < 0.1$, **: $p < 0.05$).

Results: Hypothesis 3
(n = 134)

	First Costumer					
	C2	B4	C4	B8	C7	B14
$\overline{q}_{1\_exp}$	0.58	0.60	0.57	0.63	0.62	0.65
s	0.256	0.294	0.276	0.283	0.281	0.301
U		8749		7741		8320
r		-0.032		-0.162		-0.091
p		0.715		0.049**		0.294
	Second Costumer: first costumer got product A					
	C2	B4	C4	B8	C7	B14
$\overline{q}_{2\_exp}^{A}$	0.56	0.59	0.55	0.60	0.58	0.62
s	0.289	0.295	0.297	0.305	0.298	0.328
U		8731		8073		8382
r		-0.033		-0.124		-0.082
p		0.694		0.151		0.343
	Second Costumer: first costumer got product B					
	C2	B4	C4	B8	C7	B14
$\overline{q}_{2\_exp}^{B}$	0.50	0.52	0.52	0.57	0.52	0.59
s	0.308	0.294	0.314	0.310	0.311	0.335
U		8695		8144		7868
r		-0.039		-0.114		-0.153
p		0.652		0.186		0.077*

Table 6: Paying the equivalent amount in commissions leads to the same distortion of advice as paying it in boni in all scenarios except for two. Hypothesis 3 is rejected on grounds of the carried out Mann-Whitney-U-Tests and the produced results. Even in the two cases that show a significant difference, the chosen threshold in the bonus-treatment exceeds that one of the commission-treatment. On the basis of these results there seems not to be any difference between paying commissions or boni. s revers to the standard deviation of the chosen threshold, r is the effect size $r = \frac{Z}{\sqrt{n}}$, and p is the significance level (*: $p < 0.1$, **: $p < 0.05$).

Results: Hypothesis 4
(n = 134)

	First Costumer					
	C2	B3	C4	B5	C7	B8
$\bar{q}_{1\_exp}$	0.58	0.60	0.57	0.63	0.62	0.63
s	0.256	0.291	0.276	0.272	0.281	0.283
U		8473		8007		8570
r		-0.052		-0.134		-0.056
p		0.548		0.121		0.516
	Second Costumer: first costumer got product A					
	C2	B3	C4	B5	C7	B8
$\bar{q}_{2\_exp}^{A}$	0.56	0.58	0.55	0.60	0.58	0.60
s	0.289	0.298	0.297	0.295	0.298	0.305
U		8658		8191		8682
r		-0.026		-0.108		-0.041
p		0.764		0.210		0.638
	Second Costumer: first costumer got product B					
	C2	B3	C4	B5	C7	B8
$\bar{q}_{2\_exp}^{B}$	0.50	0.51	0.52	0.54	0.52	0.57
s	0.308	0.302	0.314	0.299	0.311	0.310
U		8665		8638		8234
r		-0.025		-0.047		-0.102
p		0.773		0.589		0.237

Table 7: The same distortion of advice can be reached by paying an overall smaller amount in boni than in commissions. The Mann-Whitney-U-Tests therefore support the hypothesis that nonlinear payments to the advisor in form of boni are more effective than linear commission-payments. There is no significant difference between any of the different treatments in any scenario. s revers to the standard deviation of the chosen threshold, r is the effect size $r = \frac{z}{\sqrt{n}}$, and p is the significance level (*: $p < 0.1$, **: $p < 0.05$).

8 Appendix

8.1 MTurk Instructions

The following instructions were given to all the participants of the experiment:

PLEASE read the Instructions very carefully since your actual payment depends on the choices you make during the experiment!

For the following Experiment imagine you are an advisor who advises one of two different products (Product A and Product B) from two different firms (Firm A and Firm B) to costumers. There are different experimental treatments and in each of them you will advise **two costumers that come to you one after another**. The treatments differ in the amount of commissions and boni the firms are paying.

The currency used during this experiment is ECU (experimental currency unit) where **60 ECU = 0.5 USD**.

THE COSTUMERS

There are two different types of costumers, type A and type B. If the costumer of type A buys product A she receives 240 ECUs. If she instead buys product B she only receives 60 ECUs.

Costumers do not know whether they are of type A or of type B, but you can observe some private information that gives you a clue about their type.

Your information is as follows: For each costumer you observe the likelihood that she is of type A. This likelihood is denoted by Q, which is independent and identically distributed in the interval from 0 to 1.

If $Q = 0$ your costumer is surely of type B, needing product B.
If $Q = 0.5$ your costumer is type A or type B with equal probability, therefore it is unclear which product it needs.
If $Q = 1.0$ your costumer is surely of type A, needing product A.

During this experiment we assume that the costumers will always buy the product you advise to them to buy!

Whatever a costumer would earn in this experiment will be donated to the international child charity "A CHILD'S HOPE". For more information visit www.achildshopefoundation.org.

YOUR COMPENSATION:

Besides your compensation of 60 ECUs for completing this experiment, you can earn an **extra income**, depending on the advice you give to your clients. This extra income will be transferred to you via a bonus in MTurk after completing the experiment.

Firms have two options to reward you for selling their products.

The first instrument are **commissions**

Commissions (c_A and c_B) are paid to you by the firm whenever you advise their product to a costumer.

The second instrument are **boni**

Boni (b_A and b_B) are paid **ONLY** if you recommend the same product to **BOTH** of your clients. That is if you sell product A to your first costumer you receive the bonus only if you sell product A to your second costumer as well. The same is true for b_B.

In the end of the experiment one treatment is randomly drawn in order to determine the extra income you get, as well as the amount that is donated to the A Child's Hope Foundation.

Experimental process:

1. Firms set their commissions and boni

2. You see the commissions and boni that are paid by the different firms

3. First costumer: You observe the probability that the client needs product A (Q) and

33

recommend either product A or product B

4. First costumer: The costumer buys the recommended product

5. First costumer: You get the commission payment for the recommended product

6. Second costumer: You observe the probability that the client needs product A (Q) and recommend either product A or product B

7. Second costumer: The costumer buys the recommended product

8. Second costumer: You gets the commission payment for the recommended product and the bonus if both products recommended are the same.

For simplicity, we will record your decisions in the following way: **For every configuration of commissions and boni, we ask you to decide upon a threshold q such that every costumer with $Q < q$ will get product B and every costumer with $Q > q$ will get product A**. If $Q = q$ the client gets either product A or product B with equal probability.

You will have to answer some easy control questions in order to ensure that you understand the experimental setting. If those questions are not answered correctly you will not be approved for the HIT.

8.2 Experiment Images

Figure 1: The five control questions.

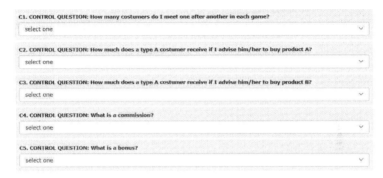

Figure 2: Example of two experiment questions with drop down list. The changed parameter was always red and bold, in order to catch the eye of the subject.

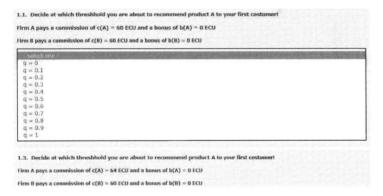

Figure 3: After completing the questions for the first costumer, the subject is informed about moving on to the second client.

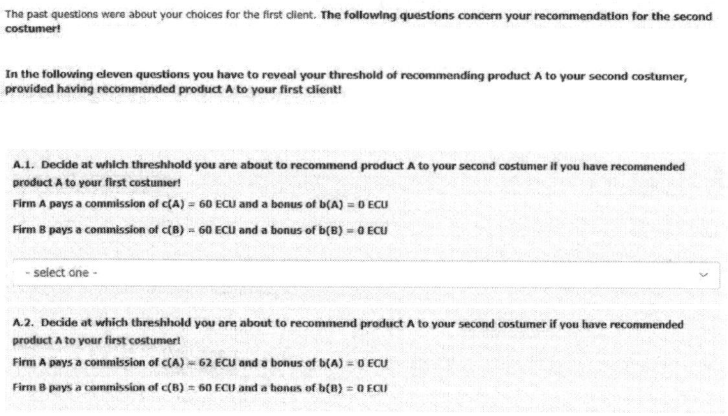

The past questions were about your choices for the first client. **The following questions concern your recommendation for the second costumer!**

In the following eleven questions you have to reveal your threshold of recommending product A to your second costumer, provided having recommended product A to your first client!

A.1. Decide at which threshhold you are about to recommend product A to your second costumer if you have recommended product A to your first costumer!

Firm A pays a commission of c(A) = 60 ECU and a bonus of b(A) = 0 ECU

Firm B pays a commission of c(B) = 60 ECU and a bonus of b(B) = 0 ECU

- select one -

A.2. Decide at which threshhold you are about to recommend product A to your second costumer if you have recommended product A to your first costumer!

Firm A pays a commission of c(A) = 62 ECU and a bonus of b(A) = 0 ECU

Firm B pays a commission of c(B) = 60 ECU and a bonus of b(B) = 0 ECU

9 Sources

Beyer, M., de Meza, D., & Reyniers, D. (2013). Do financial advisor commissions distort client choice?. *Economics Letters, 119*(2), 117-119.

Fehr, E., & Schmidt, K. (1999). A Theory of Fairness, Competition, and Cooperation. *The Quarterly Journal of Economics, 114*(3), 817-868.

Dulleck, U., & Kerschbamer, R. (2006). On doctors, mechanics, and computer specialists: The economics of credence goods. *Journal of Economic literature, 44*(1), 5-42.

Dulleck, U., Kerschbamer, R., & Sutter, M. (2011). The economics of credence goods: An experiment on the role of liability, verifiability, reputation, and competition. *The American Economic Review, 101*(2), 525-555.

Kerschbamer, R., Sutter, M., & Dulleck, U. (2016). How social preferences shape incentives in (experimental) markets for credence goods. *The Economic Journal, 127*(600), 393-416.

Goodman, J. K., Cryder, C. E., & Cheema, A. (2013). Data collection in a flat world: The strengths and weaknesses of Mechanical Turk samples. *Journal of Behavioral Decision Making, 26*, 213-224.

Halan, M., & Sane, R. (2016). Misled and mis-sold: Financial misbehaviour in retail banks?. NSEIFMR Finance Foundation Financial Deepening and Household Finance Research Initiative.

Honda, J., & Inderst, R., (2017). Nonlinear Incentives and Advisor Bias. Available at SSRN: https://ssrn.com/abstract=3088484 or http://dx.doi.org/10.2139/ssrn.3088484

Horton, J. J., Rand, D. G., & Zeckhauser, R. J. (2011). The online laboratory: Conducting experiments in a real labor market. *Experimental economics, 14*(3), 399-425.

Hung, A., Clancy, N., Dominitz, J., Talley, E., Berrebi, C. & Suvankulov, F. (2008), Investor and industry perspectives on investment advisers and broker-dealers, RAND Institute for

Civil Justice Tecnical Report.

Inderst, R. (2015). Regulating commissions in markets with advice. *International Journal of Industrial Organization, 43*, 137-141.

Inderst, R., & Ottaviani, M. (2012a). Competition through Commissions and Kickbacks. *The American Economic Review, 102*(2), 780-809.

Inderst, R., & Ottaviani, M. (2012b). Regulating financial advice. *European Business Organization Law Review (EBOR), 13*(2), 237-246.

Ipeirotis, P. (2010). Demographics of Mechanical Turk. (CeDER Working Paper-10-01). New York University. Retrieved from http://hdl.handle.net/2451/29585.

Kees, J., Berry, C., Burton, S., & Sheehan, K. (2017). An analysis of data quality: Professional panels, student subject pools, and Amazon's Mechanical Turk. *Journal of Advertising, 46*(1), 141-155.

McCredie, M. N., & Morey, L. C. (2018). Who Are the Turkers? A Characterization of MTurk Workers Using the Personality Assessment Inventory. Assessment. https://doi.org/10.-1177/1073191118760709

Mullainathan, S., Noeth, M., & Schoar, A. (2012). The market for financial advice: An audit study (No. w17929). National Bureau of Economic Research.

Paolacci, G., Chandler, J., & Ipeirotis, P. G. (2010). Running experiments on Amazon Mechanical Turk. *Judgment and Decision Making, 5*, 411–419.

Reurink, A. (2018). Financial fraud: a literature review. *Journal of Economic Surveys, 32*(5), 1292-1325.

Shapiro, D. N., Chandler, J., & Mueller, P. A. (2013). Using Mechanical Turk to study clinical populations. *Clinical Psychological Science, 1*, 213-220.

Stritch, J. M., Pedersen, M. J., & Taggart, G. (2017). The Opportunities and Limitations of Using Mechanical Turk (MTURK) in Public Administration and Management Scholarship. *International Public Management Journal, 20,* 489-511.

Druck:
Customized Business Services GmbH
im Auftrag der KNV-Gruppe
Ferdinand-Jühlke-Str. 7
99095 Erfurt